2

D0764165

To all the Mothers that usher into the universe the dawn of Hope...Thank You for your labor, love and sacrifice. -J.L.,Jr.

Dedicated to the courageous women in my family who came before me. I am your wildest dream. -M.M.

Text Copyright © 2020 by John Light Jr.
Illustration Copyright © 2020 by Monica Mikai

ISBN: 978-1-73-472634-3

Summary: Many Ancestors were responsible for bringing us into the world. My Mothers Wildest Dreams honors the Mothers responsible for bringing Mister John here.

My Mothers Wildest Dreams

Written by

John Light Jr.

Illustrated by

Monica Mikai

I am my Mothers wildest dreams.

I am the wish Grandma Hanna made as she labored to make her home safe and warm in the Old Dominion.

I am Mama Mamie's desire for her children to always find their way back to each other no matter how long they have been apart.

I am the hope Wu Wa held that one day her children would pull down pillars of hate.

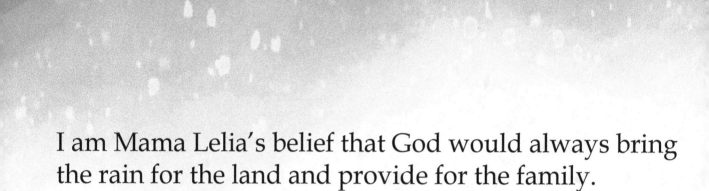

I am Mama Lelia's belief that God would always bring the rain for the land and provide for the family.

I am the anticipation that filled Grandma Ossie's heart when family visited. She always made sure good food was on the table.

I am the confidence Grandma Ruth possessed in knowing trouble does not last always.

I am my Grancy's hope that a life of love and grace will forever follow her grandchildren and great-grandchildren.

I am the answer to many nights of prayer for the strength and ability to bring forth a child.

I am my Mama's wildest dream.

CPSIA information can be obtained
at www.ICGtesting.com
Printed in the USA
LVHW070015170521
687110LV00026B/442